Treatment of Anxiety Disorders

The treatment of anxiety disorders has had a long and varied history. One may notice that history tends to repeat itself. When considering the history of anxiety treatments, four historical phases should be addressed. The pre-psychology era consists of approaches and treatments prior to 1879. The early era of psychology constitutes the period from 1879 until the end of World War II. The post-World War II era until 1980 distinguishes itself from the period of 1980 to the present in that 1980 was the first time that anxiety disorders were uniquely separated from other disorders into their own diagnostic caveat. During these various time periods, anxiety disorders were treated in a variety

of ways that were often similar in many cases to the

treatments of previous eras.

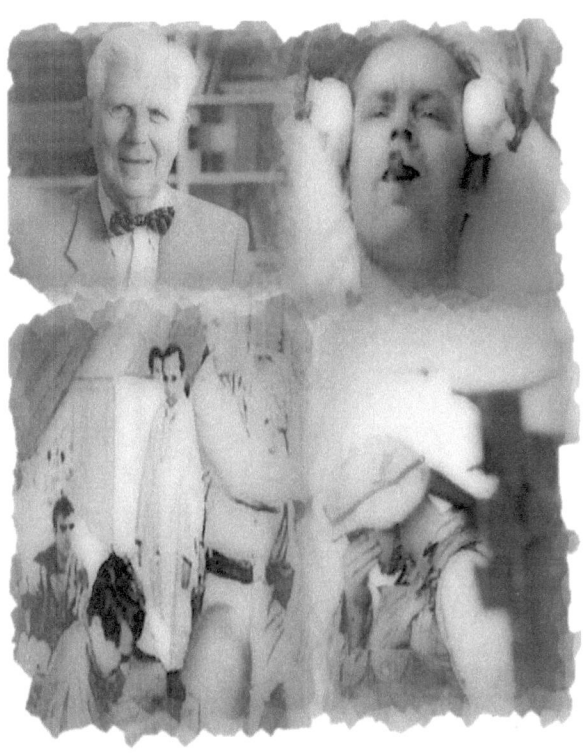

Medications have been a prevalent method

of treatment throughout history. Over time,

many of the medications have been noted to

have dangerous side effects. The use of

medications can be useful in certain

scenarios, but the hazards of medications

should be considered. During recent times,

the medicating of anxiety has been a notable

issue resulting in a great deal of research

that stands to be for and against medications.

In the current era, anxiety has been

divided into several disorders. With the

focus shifting from anxiety to specific

disorders, treatments have become

prominent for the individual disorders as opposed to anxiety as a general concept. In the case of specific phobias, systematic desensitization therapy has continued to be one of the most common treatments even though the method has been in use for over sixty years. In the case of Post Traumatic Stress Disorder (PTSD), Eye Movement Desensitization and Reprocessing (EMDR) has emerged over the last twenty years as a newer treatment that has been seen as successful in the treating of such a distressing condition.

Pre-Psychology Era Treatments

In ancient times, anxiety disorders were distressing problems very similar to how they are problems for many people today. Gabriel (1987) described one of the earliest noted treatments for anxiety was around 2000 BC when tribes in modern-day Russia ingested poisonous Amanitia mushrooms to counteract symptoms similar to PTSD-like symptoms. The mushrooms produce a euphoric state with delusions, which replace the fear and dread that is normally experienced during flashbacks. Stone (1997) explained that during the Hellenistic Period, Greeks prescribed marriage as a therapeutic treatment of anxiety. The Greeks believed that the companionship provided by marriage and family would deter the effects of general anxiety in individuals. In the ninth century, Vikings would drink deer urine, which acted as a stimulant, because it was believed to decrease reactions to stress and anxiety during and after combat (Gabriel, 1987).

Throughout the middle ages, treatments revolved around superstition and religion. Shorter (1997) described a common treatment in Europe during the middle ages was to prescribe laxatives. The reasoning behind this treatment was that mental illness could be purged from the body by defecating out the illness. During the same time period, the Turks and other Islamic countries treated anxiety by smoking hashish, which had a calming and euphoric effect. These treatments were designed to mask the symptoms of the anxiety long enough for the individuals to be functional useful to the individuals who were administering the treatments.

Upon discovering the New World, treatments for anxiety had changed very little. Havins (1976) explained how wealthy Europeans traveled great distances to treat their anxiety by visiting sacred water springs during the sixteenth and seventeenth centuries. They believed particular waters had healing powers when bathed in or drank. Meanwhile, the Inca of South America discovered by Europeans during that time period were found to chew on Coca leaves to overcome anxiety during combat. The Coca leaf is the main ingredient in the production of cocaine.

In the eighteenth century, Friedrich Scheidemantel created the first systematic text on psychosomatic medicine. Stone (1997) explained that this new approach utilized positive stimuli and experiences to counteract negative emotions and reactions. The approach was very similar to modern counter-conditioning techniques. Takashi (1993) described how another forerunner of a modern approach was being in used in Japan during the mid-nineteenth century. Dr. Genyu Imaizumi was practicing an approach to treating anxiety disorders called persuasion therapy during the 1850s. The approach was fundamentally similar to modern Cognitive Behavior Therapy (CBT) and Rational Emotive Behavioral Therapy (REBT). The nineteenth century also paved the way for some early developments in Electro-Convulsive Therapy (ECT) and pharmaceutical treatments. Shorter (1997) explained that Rest Therapy that was practiced in the mid-nineteenth century consisted of bed rest, a milk diet, massage, and electrical shock. Rest therapy, therefore, served as one of the earliest treatments to utilize electricity for the treatment of anxiety. Potassium Bromide, the forerunner of Barbital and Phenobarbital, was developed in during the same century as a start to the practice of medicating individuals with anxiety disorders (Hecht. 2010).

The Early Era of Psychology

Psychology can trace its roots as a science to 1879 when the first psychology lab was founded. One can also note shifts in how anxiety was treated due to the shift to a scientific approach to understanding psychological mechanisms. In the early years of psychology, psychoanalysis was the dominant approach among therapists to treating many disorders including anxiety. The approach consisted of having the individual reflect upon the underlying causes to his or her problems. The psychoanalyst would have the individual make connections between their current emotions and unresolved events from earlier in life. The goal was to have the client work through their issues in an attempt to resolve unsettled issues.

In addition to psychoanalysis, Electrical Shock Therapy was commonly used to treat anxiety disorders (Gabriel, 1987). Mankad, Beyer, Weiner, and Krystal (2010) reported that there has been no evidence that ECT treatments produce benefits to individuals who suffer from anxiety. Many psychiatrists of the time were heavily reliant on ECT for treatment regardless of the lack of supporting evidence for its effectiveness in treating anxiety. In addition to ECT treatments, Paul Dubois introduced the concept of persuasion therapy to Europe in the early twentieth century in a manner that was coupled with psychoanalysis. This approach was utilized in treating individuals with phobias and other symptoms associated with anxiety disorders (Robertson, 2010).

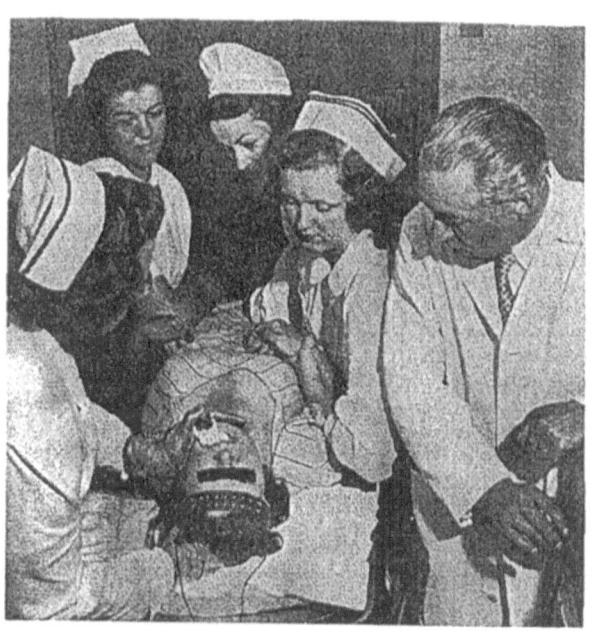

During the World Wars, a variety of treatments for PTSD emerged that could be seen as highly questionable today. The

questionable approaches can be seen as stemming from the denial of PTSD as a legitimate condition during these time periods. Herman (1997) provided several examples including the use of tranquilizers, placebos, and the surgical implantation of metal balls in the larynx of soldiers during WWI. The tranquilizers were used by the Russians and served to make the soldiers functional enough to return to the front lines with little to no resolution to the soldier's symptoms. The placebos were used to make the soldiers think that they were getting treatment. The metal balls placed in the larynx allowed soldiers who had suffered from trauma that resulted an inability to

speak to make sounds when they attempted

to scream in terror from the flashbacks that

were a result of their trauma.

During World War II, the stigma of

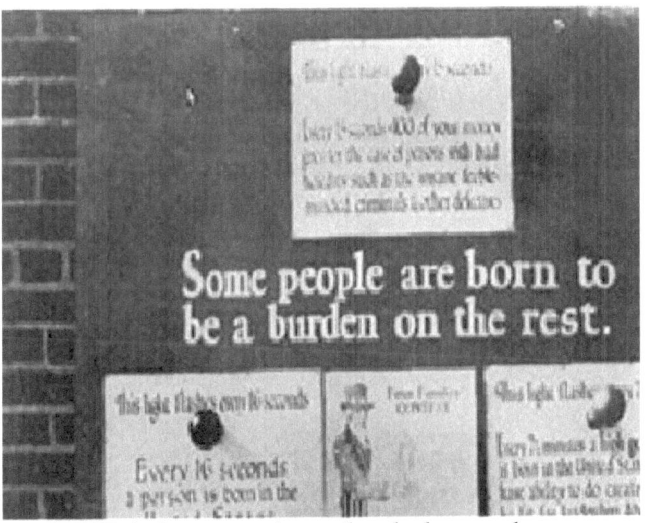

PTSD being experienced only by weak

individuals was still present, but the

increasing psychological causalities brought attention to the condition as being something more than a symptom of being weak. During the war, several clinicians attempted to treat anxiety using a variety of approaches. Captain Joseph Campbell, a military doctor, treated patients with an approach including rest, work, and a form of brief psychoanalysis. Meanwhile, others used a mixture of hypnosis, drugs, and cathartic reliving of traumatic experiences (Herman, 1997).

The Post-World War II Era

With the end of World War II, research, funding, and ideas about treating anxiety disorders increased greatly.

Systematic desensitization was introduced in the early fifties as a method involving the gradual exposure of individuals to stimuli related to their anxiety and previous trauma (Hunt, 1988). This approach was the product of the behaviorist movement to break away from the inconsistency of psychoanalytic and psychodynamic approaches. Cognitive approaches to treatment also began to develop after the behavioral approach became popular. REBT was introduced as a therapeutic approach to treat anxiety in the late fifties and continued to grow in popularity for decades (Prochaska and

Norcross, 2009). ECT treatments were reintroduced as Cranial Electrotherapy Stimulation (CES) in Russia in the fifties using lower voltages of electricity than previous ECT treatments (Hunt, 1988). As CES began to become popular, it quickly diminished with rise of the anti-psychiatry movement that developed in the sixties.

As the cognitive revolution brought about therapies such as REBT and CBT in the sixties, another revolution was starting up among the individuals that treated anxiety disorders. This second revolution was the medication revolution. From the end of the sixties to the beginning of the eighties, Valium was the most prescribed drug in America (Stolerman, 2010). During 1979, three billion prescriptions were written for Valium worldwide. Medications such as Valium, Chlordiazepoxide, Propranolol, and the Tricyclic Antidepressants were the answer to anxiety disorders during the much of the sixties and seventies.

The Modern Era

The actual defining of the disorders in the DSM-III marks the beginning of the modern era of treatment of anxiety disorders. Until the DSM-III, anxiety disorders did not have their own section and many were not recognized as distinct disorders (American Psychiatric Association, 1952, 1968, 1980). Many of the prior treatments viewed anxiety disorders as symptoms of other disorders because anxiety disorders were not seen as unique disorders until the publication of the DSM-III. With the modern era of anxiety treatments, one can note that the treatments have become a more specific to treating anxiety as opposed to treating irrelevant symptoms that are not associated with anxiety as had been defined in prior diagnostic manuals.

The medication revolution of the sixties and seventies did not stop with the defining of anxiety disorders. Various other medications were developed during the eighties and into the nineties such as Xanax, Prozac, Zoloft, and Paxil. The medications have created a great deal of controversy due to increased awareness concerning their side effects. These side effects include suicidal ideation in adults and children, high rates of dependence, withdraw, cognitive impairments, and physiological responses (Stolerman, 2010). Over the past three decades, the medicating of individuals with anxiety disorders has begun to be seen as problematic for the patients. Berman, Jones, and McCloskey (2005) found the use of diazepam or Valium to be correlated with self-aggressive and suicidal behavior.

Deakin, Aitken, Dowson, Robbins, and Sahakian (2004) found that diazepam produced impairments in cognitive functioning such as decision-making and planning tasks.

The newer medications have also been scrutinized due their side effects.

Bardhi, Sifaneck, Johnson, and Dunlap (2007) found that Alpraxolam, which is most frequently known by the brand name Xanax, was becoming so widely abused that it was commonly being used as an alternative to cocaine and marijuana among drug subcultures. Williams and Wooltorton (2005) found that the use of Paroxetine or Paxil during the first trimester of pregnancy was linked to a variety of birth defects in the unborn child. Even with the mounting evidence of the dangerous side effects of the medications, these prescriptions are still being given to individuals suffering from anxiety disorders such as PTSD,

Generalized Anxiety Disorder (GAD), Panic

Disorders, and even Specific Phobias.

With the defining of anxiety

disorders, Cognitive Behavioral Therapy

(CBT) became the most popular

psychotherapeutic approach to treating

anxiety disorders in the eighties. As of

today, CBT is still the most commonly used approach in treating anxiety (Prochaska and Norcross, 2009). CBT is an approach that attempts to break down the irrational beliefs that lead to anxiety. In breaking down the irrational beliefs, CBT attempts to restructure the thought processes of the individual so that the power of fear is taken away from the source of anxiety whether it be related to a specific object, event, person, task, or concept. In the case of GAD, CBT often focuses on the concept of worry in general through a process of restructuring the individual's entire thought process so that they may dismiss the anxiety as being irrational and unfounded. This process

results in the individual being able to

overcome their worry (Andrews, 2004).

Systematic desensitization has

served as an integral part of CBT treatments.

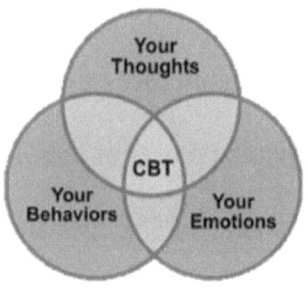

Gradual desensitization processes have

received continual support as an effective as

a treatment of anxiety disorders that has be

in common use over the last sixty years as

was in use as an independent treatment of

anxiety prior to the creation of CBT.

Systematic desensitization is one of the most

common treatments of Specific Phobias. The

process of systematic desensitization

involves first developing trust between the

therapist and client. Without trust, the client

would be unlikely to open up to the

therapist. The client is then trained in

relaxation techniques such as controlled

breathing and deep muscle relaxation. In

controlled breathing, the individual is

trained in methods of slowing their rate of

respiration. Deep muscle relaxation involves

the tensing and relaxing of specific muscle

groups. Through deep muscle relaxation, the

individual will become aware of when he or she contracts muscle groups as a response to experienced anxiety. These techniques will be used during exposure to the stimuli that produces anxiety (Andrews, 2004).

Where the magic happens

Your comfort zone

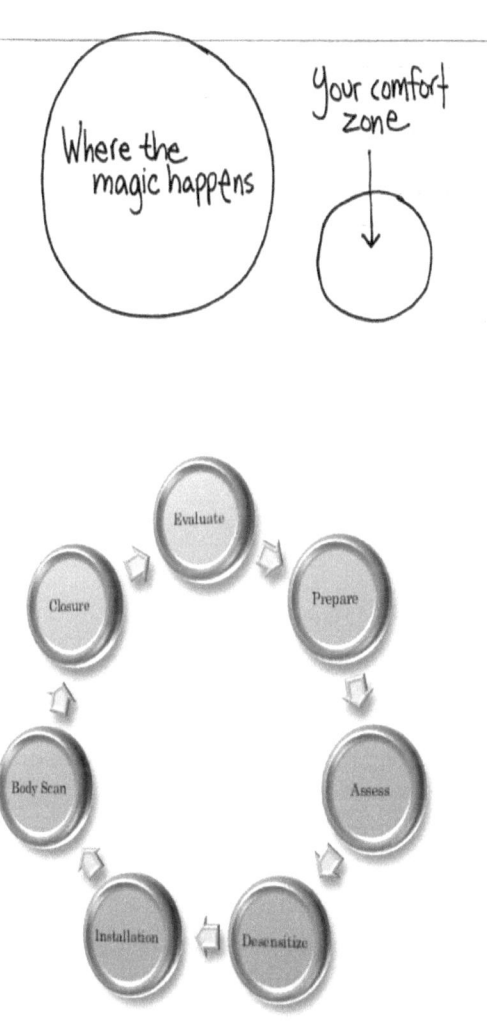

The exposure of the individual to the stimulus that produces the anxiety is a process of exposure in varying degrees of increased strength. In many cases, the early exposure will be simulated through imagining the threatening experience or object. The length of simulated exposure will gradually increase over time and repeated experiences. Each time the individual is exposed to the threat, the client will use relaxation techniques to counter-condition their response to the stimulus until they reach a base line rate of anxiety. There are several mitigating factors that can be used to graduate the exposure. These factors can include distance, duration, activities done while exposed, and whether the individual is alone or with someone while exposed to the threat (Andrews, 2004). As the individual reaches their base rate of anxiety, they should reflect on how their response was different than originally expected. The reflection on their response will serve to reinforce the experience of overcoming the fear. Over time, the individual will gradually be able to confront their fear in reality for longer periods of time until they are desensitized to the fear-producing stimulus (Caske, Herman, and Vansteenwegen, 2006).

Virtual Reality Exposure Therapy (VRET) has emerged over the course of the last decade as an alternative to traditional live exposure therapy (Meyerbroker and Emmelkamp, 2010). VRET has been found to be as effective in treating anxiety disorders such as Specific Phobias and PTSD as classical exposure therapies (Opris et al., 2012; McLay et al., 2012; Wald and

Taylor, 2003). VRET has been used with Vietnam War Veterans in most studies. In the treatment, the individual re-experiences similar trauma and trauma triggers through the use of a head-mounted display or they will enter a room with computer-generated imagery that is projected onto the walls of the room. The virtual simulations are conducted in a similar to fashion to *in vivo* exposures. Such methods of exposure are useful in treating individual with PTSD due to the dangers associated with the original trauma that was experienced. In addition, some advanced exposures in treating

Specific Phobias can get a good degree of
use from VRET.

Over the last twenty years, Eye
Movement Desensitization and
Reprocessing (EMDR) has become a
popular treatment for PTSD (Dworkin,
2005). Shapiro (2001) explained that EMDR
allowed individuals to recall traumatic
experiences while reprocessing the
experience in a cognitive manner so that
experience does not linger with the person.
In the treatment, the reprocessing of the
experience reduces the influence of the past
event upon the current cognitive processes
of the individual. EMDR consists of the

client focusing on an image of the traumatic experience that resulted in his or her PTSD. During this time, the client gives attention to the related emotions, thoughts, and sensations that are negatively associated with the image. The client will then be instructed by the therapist to perform lateral eye movements that scan the across the individuals entire visual. The individual will continue to scan their visual field until they are desensitized. Once desensitized to the image, the client will focus on his or her body to note any type of physiological responses or changes. At the end of the session, the therapist will discuss the possibility of the client becoming aware of new information about the traumatic event. (Lipke, 2000).

EMDR serves as a method of desensitizing the individual to the cognitive cues that were associated with the previously experienced trauma. As the individual is desensitized to the cues, the client finally processes the information from the traumatic experience that was continuously being relived through flashbacks, night terrors, and physiological arousal associated with the trauma. The avoiding of stimuli associated with the trauma perpetuates the symptoms due the individual avoiding stimuli that would allow them to cognitively process the traumatic experience and associated stimuli and cognitions. Once the lingering emotions and cognitions are processed, a possibility exists that other unprocessed memories about the traumatic event may arise to allow the individual to become aware of them. It is common for therapists that use EMDR to assign a thought journal for the client to maintain for the purpose of noting any new memories of the traumatic events for future sessions (Shapiro, 2002). The process of sensation processing coupled with desensitization to the stimuli will then be

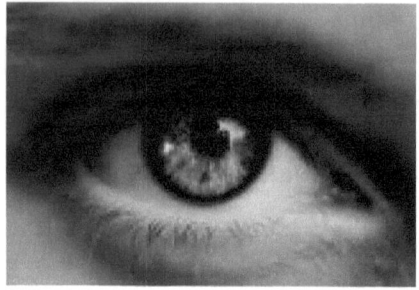 repeated with any new memories of the traumatic events to allow the client to process associated stimuli.

Summary

The treatment of anxiety disorders has developed over the course of four thousand years with many changes and many times in which history has repeated itself. The earliest treatments of anxiety involved the consumption of poisonous substances. Today, individuals still consume substances that could be hazardous to their health to treat the symptoms of their anxiety. In the case of some medication, abuse commonly occurs that advances the dangers associated with such medications. Some of the side effects of modern medications can be seen as more harmful than the disorder is at times. Persuasion therapy served as the theoretical foundation of many of today's modern therapies such as CBT. Systematic desensitization can be seen as a parallel to some of the early psychoanalytical approaches that focused on reliving the trauma for the purpose of working through their issues. With each new approach, science gives old treatments new names and occasionally creates a new approach that is different but has connections to some of the earlier approaches.

As the anxiety disorders have been divided into specific disorders, research focus on creating specific treatments for the particular disorders as opposed to label all anxiety under one umbrella disorder. In clearly defining the type of anxiety disorder, better treatments and interventions may provided to the client as opposed to inappropriate treatments. Some of the newer treatments, such as EMDR and VRET, have the potential to advance psychologists' understanding of how these specific disorders can be approached and the quality of life can be improved for the individuals that suffer from them. Further research into the use of advanced technologies and advances in the understanding of how individuals are affected by such treatments could strengthen the standing of such approaches or allow them to be more focused on the particular cases in which they are the most effective methods of treatment.

References

American Psychiatric Association. (1952).

> *Diagnostic and Statistical Manual of
> Mental Disorders.* Washington, DC:
> Author.

American Psychiatric Association. (1968).

> *Diagnostic and Statistical Manual of
> Mental Disorders (2nd ed.).* Washington,
> DC: Author.

American Psychiatric Association. (1980).

> *Diagnostic and Statistical Manual of
> Mental Disorders (3rd ed.).* Washington,
> DC: Author.

Andrews, J. (2004). *Management of Mental
> Disorders (4th Ed.).* New York, NY:
> Cambridge University Press.

Bardhi, F., Sifaneck, S. J., Johnson, B. D., & Dunlap,
E. (2007). Pills, thrills and bellyaches:
Case studies of prescription pill use and
misuse among marijuana/blunt smoking
middle class young women.
Contemporary Drug Problems, 34(1), 53-
101.

Berman, M. E., Jones, G. D., & McCloskey, M. S.
(2005). The effects of diazepam on
human self-aggressive behavior.
Psychopharmacology, 178(1), 100-106.
doi:10.1007/s00213-004-1966-8

Craske, M., Hermans, D., & Vansteenwegen, D.
(2006). *Fear and Learning: From Basic
Processes to Clinical Implications.*
Washington, DC: American

Psychological Association.

Deakin, J. B., Aitken, M. F., Dowson, J. H., Robbins,

T. W., & Sahakian, B. J. (2004).

Diazepam produces disinhibitory

cognitive effects in male volunteers.

Psychopharmacology, 173(1/2), 88-97.

Dworkin, M. (2005). *EMDR and the Relational

Imperative.* New York, NY: Taylor and

Francis Group.

Gabriel, R. (1987). *No More Heroes: Madness &

Psychiatry in War.* New York, NY: Hill

and Wang.

Havins, P. (1976). *The Spas of England.* London,

UK: Robert Hale and Company.

Herman, J. (1997). *Trauma and Recovery: The*

Aftermath of Violence- From Domestic
Abuse to Political Terror. New York,
NY: W. H. Freeman and Company.

Hecht, A. (2010). *Understanding Drugs:*
Antidepressants and Antianxiety Drugs.
New York, NY: Chelsea House
Publishers.

Hunt, D. (1988). *No More Fears.* New York, NY:
Warner Books.

Lipke, H. (2000). *EMDR and Psychotherapy*
Integration. Boca Raton, FL: CRC Press,
LLC.

McLay, R. N., Graap, K., Spira, J., Perlman, K.,
Johnston, S., Rothbaum, B. O., & ...
Rizzo, A. (2012). Development and

Testing of Virtual Reality Exposure Therapy for Post-Traumatic Stress Disorder in Active Duty Service Members Who Served in Iraq and Afghanistan. *Military Medicine, 177*(6), 635-642.

Meyerbröker, K., & Emmelkamp, P. G. (2010). Virtual reality exposure therapy in anxiety disorders: a systematic review of process-and-outcome studies. *Depression & Anxiety, 27*(10), 933-944.

Mankad, M., Beyer, J., Weiner, R., and Krystal, A. (2010) *Clinical Manual of Electroconvulsive Therapy.* Wasshington, DC: American Psychiatric Publishing Inc.

Opriş, D., Pintea, S., García-Palacios, A., Botella, C.,

    Szamosközi, Ş., & David, D. (2012).

    Virtual reality exposure therapy in

    anxiety disorders: a quantitative meta-

    analysis. *Depression & Anxiety, 29*(2),

    85-93. doi:10.1002/da.20910

Porter, R. (1997). *Medicine, A History of Healing:*

    Ancient Traditions to Modern Practices.

    New York, NY: The Ivy Press.

Prochaska, J. and Norcross, J. (2009) *Systems of*

    Psychotherapy: A Transtheoretical

    Analysis. Belmont, CA: Cengage

    Learning

Roberson, D. (2010). *The Philosophy of Cognitive-*

    Behavioral Therapy. London, UK: The

    Studio Publishing Services.

Shapiro, F. (2001). *Eye Movement Desensitization and Reprocessing (EMDR) Basic Principles, Protocols, and Procedures.* New York, NY: The Guilford Press.

Shapiro, F. (2002). *EMDR as an Integrative Psychotherapy Approach.* Washington, DC: American Psychological Association.

Sheehan, D. (1986). *The Anxiety Disease.* New York, NY: Bantam Books.

Shorter, E. (1998). *A History of Psychiatry: From the Era of the Asylum to the Age of Prozac.* New York, NY: John Wiley and Sons, Inc.

Stone, M. (1997). *Healing the Mind: A History of*

Psychiatry from Antiquity to the Present.
London, United Kingdom: Pimlico.

Stolerman, I. (2010). *Encyclopedia of
Psychopharmacology.* London, UK:
Springer Books.

Takahashi, T. (1993). A persuasion therapy for panic
disorder in old Japanese medical literature.
Comprehensive Psychiatry, 34(1), 31-35.
doi:10.1016/0010-440X(93) 90032-Y

Wald, J., & Taylor, S. (2003). Preliminary Research
on the Efficacy of Virtual Reality Exposure
Therapy to Treat Driving Phobia.
Cyberpsychology & Behavior, 6(5), 459.
doi:10.1089/109493103769710488

Williams, M., & Wooltorton, E. (2005). Paroxetine
(Paxil) and congenital malformations.

CMAJ: Canadian Medical Association Journal, 173(11), 1320-1321.

doi:10.1503/cmaj.051421